LIGHT SURELY TRAVELS FAST!

SCIENCE BOOK OF EXPERIMENTS

CHILDREN'S SCIENCE EDUCATION BOOKS

Speedy Publishing LLC
40 E. Main St. #1156
Newark, DE 19711
www.speedypublishing.com

In this book, we're going to talk about the properties of light and experiments with light. So, let's get right to it!

WHAT IS LIGHT?

Light is quite mysterious. It doesn't have any mass. In fact, scientists say that it isn't a type of matter at all. Light is an energy form. Sound is a type of wave and sometimes light behaves like a wave.

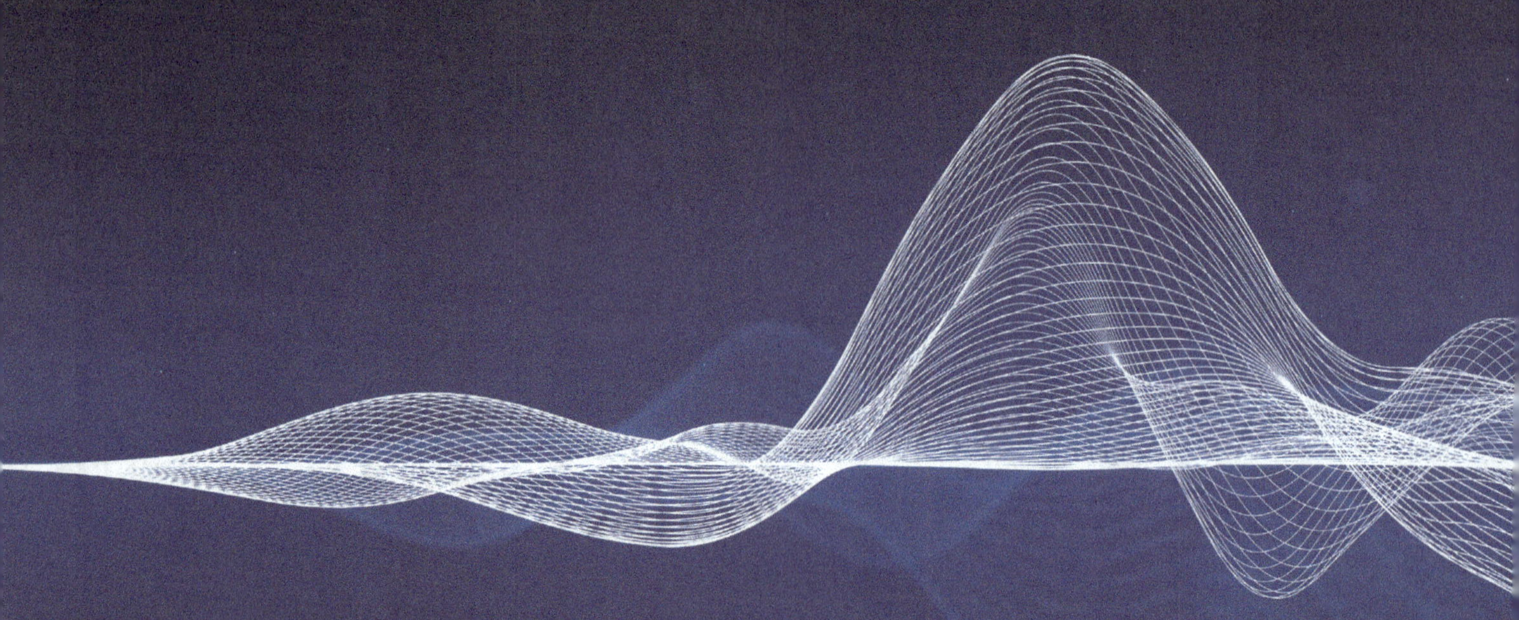

LIGHT WAVE

However, some of its properties are more like the properties of particles. Light is made out of photons and sometimes they behave like particles and sometimes they behave like waves. This theory that light behaves as a wave and also as a particle is called the theory of wave-particle duality.

WHAT IS A PHOTON?

Light is composed of particles called photons. Photons don't have any mass or electrical charge. They're stable, but they can also interact with different kinds of particles.

LIGHT IMAGED AS BOTH A PARTICLE AND WAVE

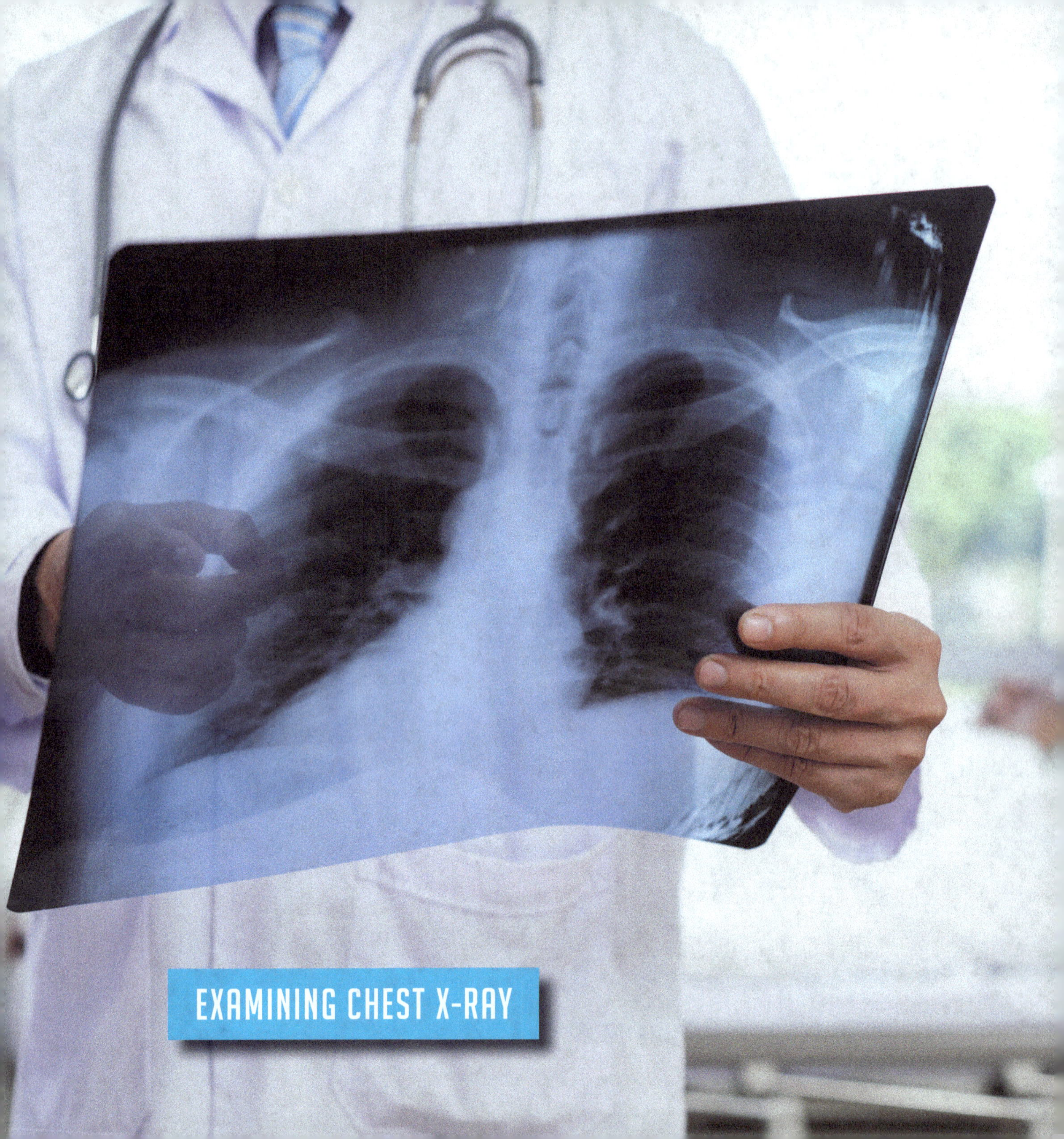

EXAMINING CHEST X-RAY

For example, they can interact with electrons. Light isn't the only type of energy made up of photons. Radio waves as well as X-rays and microwaves are composed of photons too.

LIGHT INTERACTS WITH MATTER

One of the reasons that scientists say that light behaves like particles is because sometimes the photons in light interact with matter. For example, if you have an asphalt road and the sun's light is bearing down on it, the energy of the photons in the light gets absorbed by the road and is let off as heat.

ASPHALT ROAD

Sometimes when matter absorbs the energy produced by photons, it ends up emitting electrons. Solar energy works on this principle. A solar cell catches the energy from these photons and changes it into electricity for use in your home.

OPAQUE OR NOT OPAQUE

Light behaves in a different way depending on the type of matter it encounters. Light can pass through both air and water. When light can travel through something, we call that type of matter "transparent." Sometimes objects reflect light.

When something is solid and light doesn't pass through it, it reflects light. This type of object is called "opaque." Some objects are solid but they let some light through and reflect some light as well. These types of objects are "translucent."

HOW WAS THE SPEED OF LIGHT FOUND?

In 1638, Galileo Galilei was the first scientist who tried to determine the speed of light. His experiments were set up on land. He and his assistant both had lamps they could cover and uncover. Galileo would take his lamp and uncover it and as soon as his assistant saw the light, he would follow suit and uncover his lamp.

GALILEO GALILEI

Galileo reasoned that he could measure the amount of time it took for him to see the lamp from his assistant and measure the distance that the light had traveled. It was a good idea but the water clocks they were using weren't accurate enough.

Galileo didn't think that light traveled at an infinite speed, but he knew to human perception it seemed to happen in an instant.

LAMP

AIRPLANES IN FORMATION

Galileo concluded that light must travel at least ten times the speed of sound. Eventually, it was discovered that the speed of sound at sea level is about 761 miles per hour, while the speed of light is a whopping 670,616, 629 miles per hour! We now have jets that can fly faster than the speed of sound, but we don't have jets that can travel the speed of light!

In 1676, the Danish astronomer Olaus Roemer came up with an experiment that he thought could determine the speed of light. His experiment was based on the eclipses of one of Jupiter's moons, the one called Io. He observed that as Earth's orbit around the sun was bringing it closer to Jupiter, Io's eclipses of its planet became shorter instead of the time predicted that it would take for Io to orbit Jupiter.

OLAUS ROEMER

THE PLANET JUPITER

On the other hand, when Earth's orbital path was at a larger distance from Jupiter, Io's eclipses of Jupiter took longer. The range of time difference was about 7 minutes. He realized that the time it would take for Io to orbit Jupiter should be the same in either case. He reasoned that the difference in time must be due to how long it was taking for the light to reach Earth.

The speed of the Earth during its orbit was already known, so the distance the Earth had traveled between the eclipses could be found. Light's speed could then be estimated based on the 7-minute time difference. Roemer measured the speed of light to be about 140,000 miles per second, but he was still off by quite a bit.

SUN AND NINE PLANETS ORBITING

ALBERT EINSTEIN

It was 1975 after numerous experiments and measurements that it was determined that the exact speed of light is 186,282 miles in one second of time! According to scientific work done by physicist Albert Einstein, nothing is capable of traveling faster than light can travel. This measurement is how fast light travels in a vacuum, which is space that doesn't have any matter in it.

Photons from the sun travel the 92.96 million miles from the sun to Earth in about 8 minutes and 20 seconds! Wow! That's fast! Light only travels at this maximum speed when it's traveling through the vacuum of space or in artificially created vacuums on Earth. When light travels through air it travels a little slower and through water it travels slower yet.

THE SUN

REFRACTION

Most of the time, rays of sunlight travel in a straight line. However, when light passes through different types of transparent materials such as water, it angles. That's true when light passes through glass. No matter what type of material it's passing through, the light's wavelength will be altered but not its frequency.

The light will change directions and bend. This occurrence is called refraction. A prism is a great example of refraction in action. As a beam of light hits a prism, the light bends and splits into different colors.

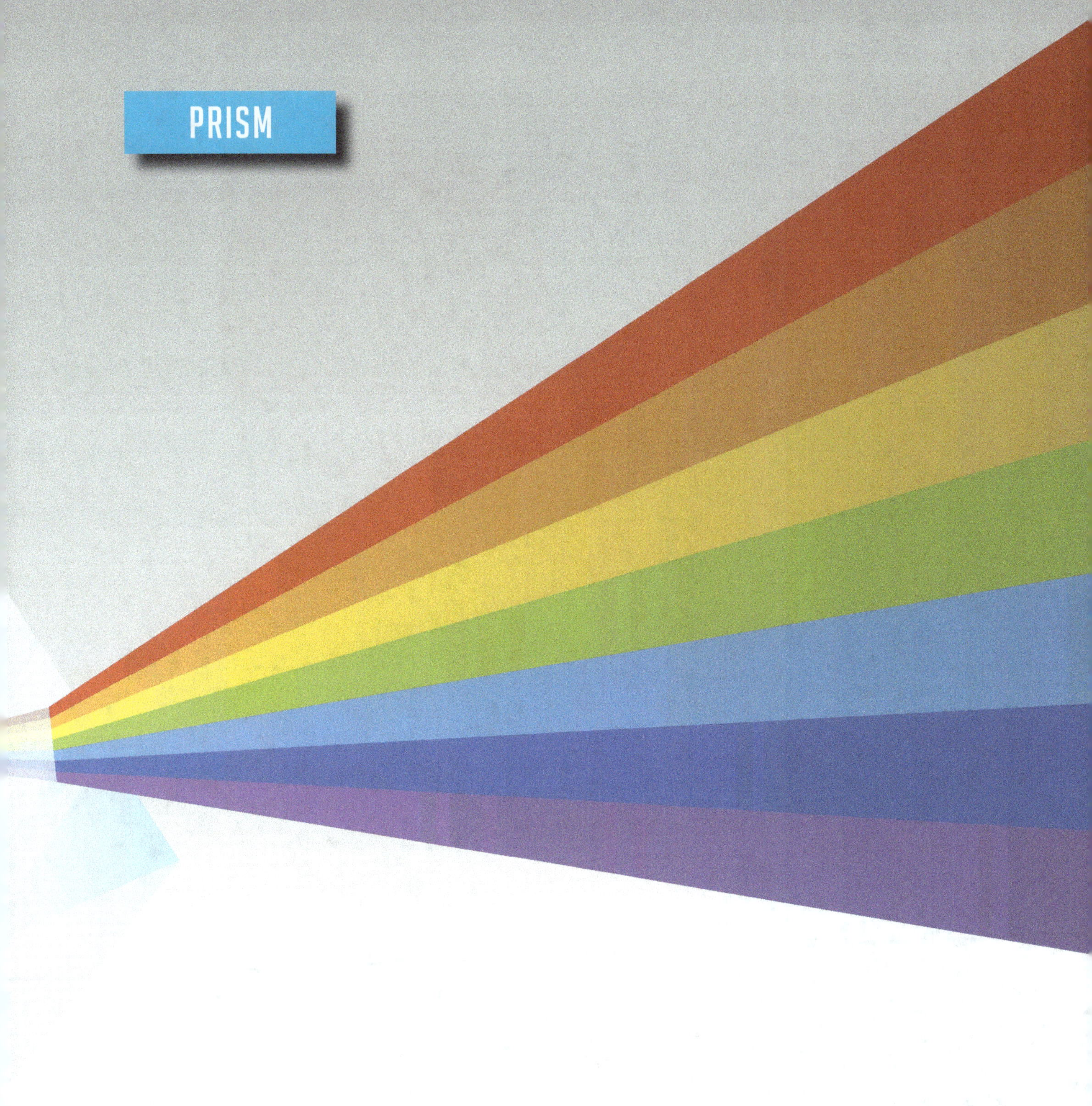
PRISM

BALLOONS

LIGHT EXPERIMENT 1

For this experiment you'll need to be outside. You'll need balloons, pins, flags, and orange cones to mark your positions. You'll take turns. One person goes to one of the orange cone positions with a balloon and a pin. The other person has just a flag.

Signal with the flag when you are ready for the other person to pop the balloon they are holding. You are carefully observing that you see the person pop the balloon before you hear it. Take turns doing this at different distances. The farther away you are, the longer of a time difference there will be between when you see the balloon pop and when you hear it.

ORANGE CONE

MULTICOLORED THUMBTACKS

The light that makes it possible for you to see the balloon popping is much faster than the sound of the balloon popping.

A natural example of this occurs when we see lightning but don't hear the thunder it produces until quite a few seconds after it.

LIGHT EXPERIMENT 2

To do this experiment, you'll need a large, flat chocolate bar and a small- to medium-sized tabletop microwave. You can measure the speed of light at home with a large flat bar of chocolate and your microwave.

CHOCOLATE BAR

MICROWAVE

A microwave uses microwave light to cook your food. This light comes out in waves that go up and down. This is why you may have noticed that food you take out of your microwave is sometimes hot in spots and sometimes not. That's why a rotating plate is needed in a microwave.

To do this experiment you need to take out the part of the microwave that makes the plate rotate. Now put the flat bar of chocolate on the plate and microwave it on high for 15 seconds. When you take the bar out, you'll notice that some parts are melted and some are not.

INSIDE OF A MICROWAVE

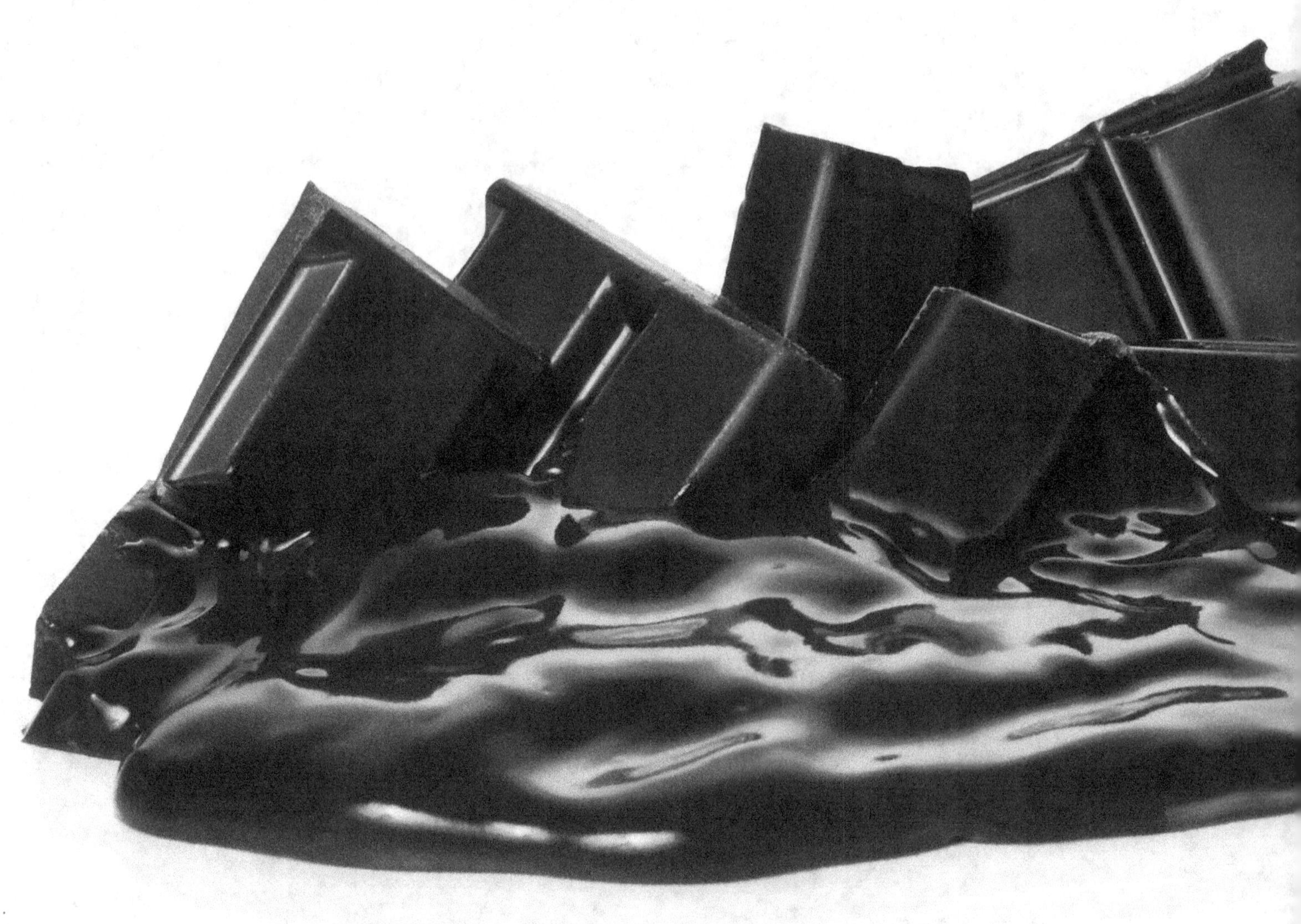

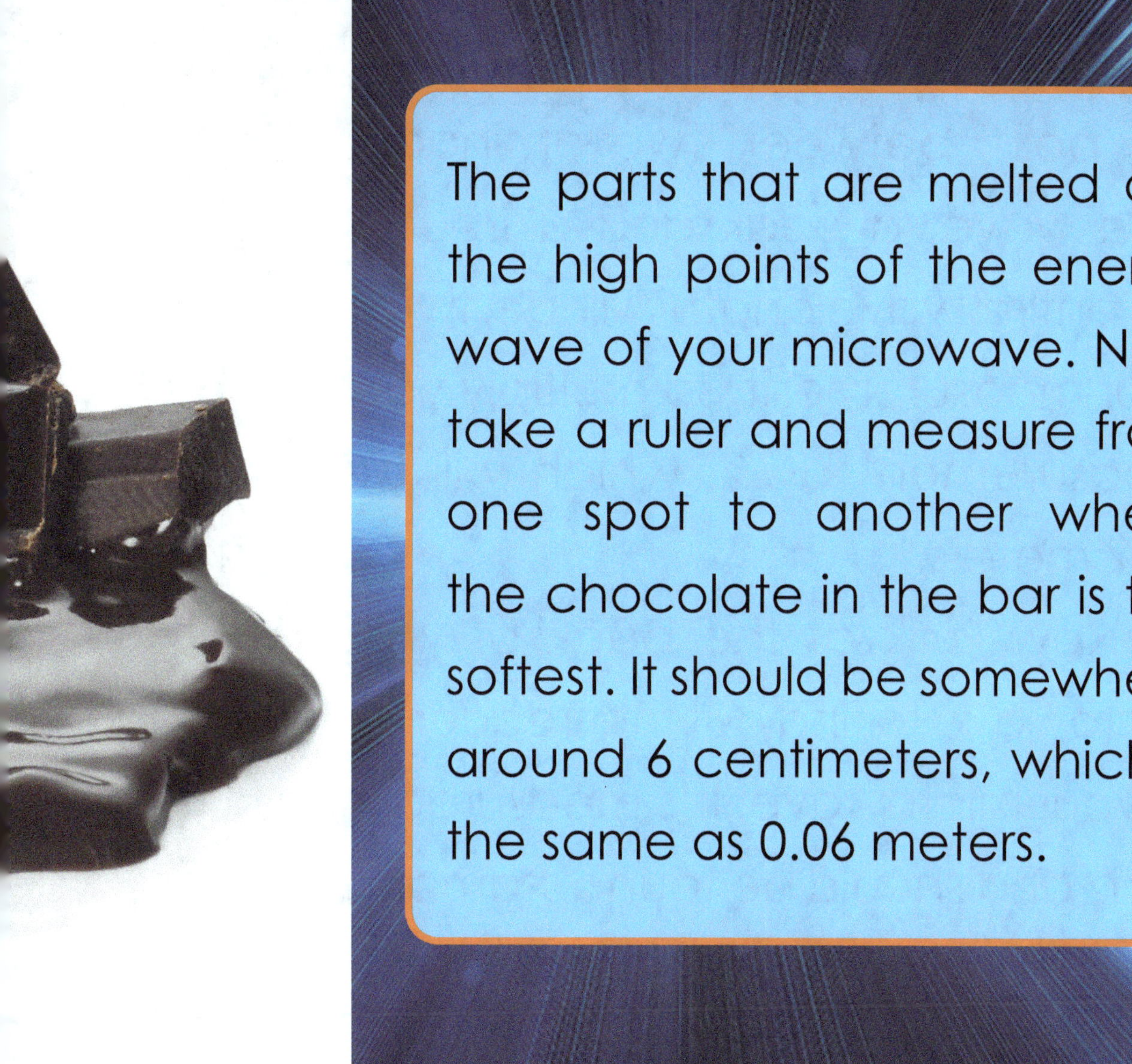

The parts that are melted are the high points of the energy wave of your microwave. Now take a ruler and measure from one spot to another where the chocolate in the bar is the softest. It should be somewhere around 6 centimeters, which is the same as 0.06 meters.

But, what you're measuring here is the point between two antinodes of a wave, a peak and a trough. An entire wavelength will be twice your measurement, so multiply your measurement by 2, which will be 0.12 meters.

Now look at the back of your microwave to find out the frequency of your microwave. It's measured in hertz and should be found stamped on the back of your microwave.

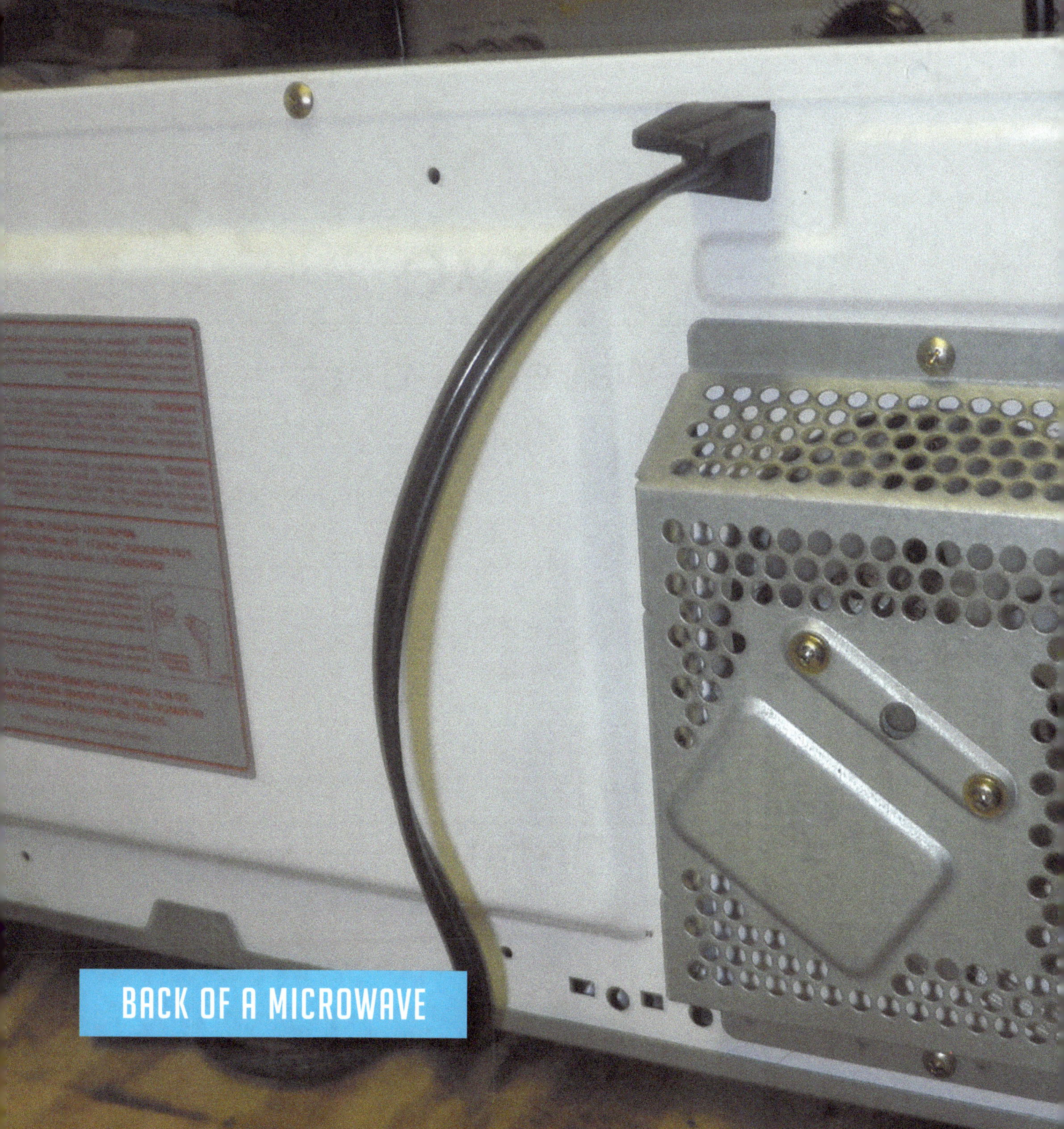

BACK OF A MICROWAVE

Wave

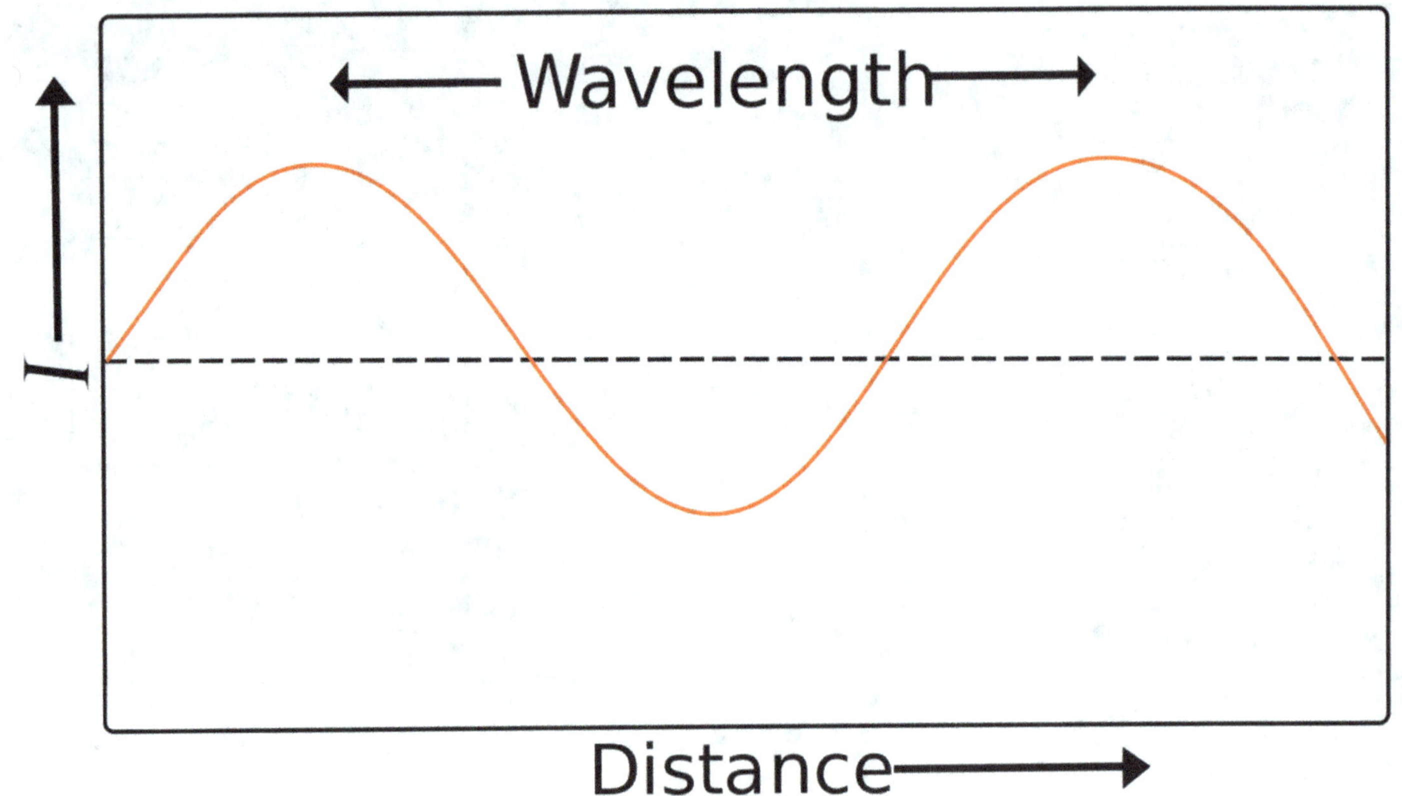

A megahertz is equivalent to 1 million hertz. So, for example if your microwave says 2,450 megahertz that's that same as 2,450 x 1,000,000 to get the hertz which is 2,450,000,000 Hz. Now multiply that frequency times the wavelength to get the speed of light:

2,450,000,000 Hz x 0.12 meters =
294,000,000 meters per second.

This is pretty close! The actual measurement is 299,792,458 meters per second, which is the same as 186,282 miles in one second. Remember there are 1609.34 meters in one mile. You measured the speed of light using your microwave and chocolate! Now you can have a bite of chocolate as your reward.

Awesome! Now you know more about the properties of light. You can find more Science Education books from Baby Professor by searching the website of your favorite book retailer.

Visit
BABY PROFESSOR
EDUCATION KIDS
www.BabyProfessorBooks.com
to download Free Baby Professor eBooks
and view our catalog of new and exciting
Children's Books

www.ingramcontent.com/pod-product-compliance
Lightning Source LLC
LaVergne TN
LVHW060506170826
845677LV00026B/1634

* 9 7 9 8 8 6 9 4 3 3 5 7 2 *